I Love You Terribly

T0079902

I Love You Terribly

Six Plays

Claudia Barnett

Carnegie Mellon University Press
Pittsburgh 2012

Acknowledgments

The author extends her gratitude to the editors of the following publications in which some of these plays first appeared:

Atlantic Pacific Press 3: "Eden."
Best Scenes for Two for the 21st Century: "Henry." (excerpt)
River Styx 80: "Sex Lessons."
Santa Clara Review 98.1: "Till Death."

Some of these plays received first productions as follows:
"Eden": Independent Actors Theatre, 2010. Directed by Emily Rollie.
"I Love You Terribly" (radio): Shoestring Radio Theatre, 2010. Directed by
        Virginia Handley.
"I Love You Terribly" (stage): Stratton Players, 2011.
"Sex Lessons": Independent Actors Theatre, 2011. Directed by Amy Darnell.
"Till Death": East Haddam Stage Company, 2008. Directed by Kandie Carle.

"Henry," "Eden" and "I Love You Terribly" were workshopped at the Mid-America Theatre Conference Playwriting Symposium (2007, 2008, 2010). I am grateful to the following actors, directors, dramaturgs, respondents, and symposia chairs for their contributions to the development of these scripts: Penelope Walrath Cole, Jon Herbert, Annaliisa Ahlman, Paul Bernstein, Andy Bragen, Eric Coble, Laura Crockarell, Sarah Crockarell, Season Ellison, Thom Davis, Cindy Gendrich, Frank Higgins, Shirley Huston-Findley, Nancy Jones, Robin Stone.

For their support of these plays, thanks to Artistic Directors Ross Brooks, Kandie Carle, Shawna Mefferd Kelty and Emily Rollie, as well as Tom Strawman, Kelly Hays, and the English Department and Faculty Research & Creative Activity Committee at Middle Tennessee State University.

Book Design: Geoffrey Dobbs

For Gaylord

CONTENTS

EDEN

CHARACTERS

ADAM	PAJAMAS.
EVE	BUSINESS SUIT.

Scene
A garden with an apple tree (or two, or six). Lots of apples.

AT RISE. EVE is on her way to work.

ADAM
It's not your fault.

EVE
I know.

ADAM
What do you mean—I know?

EVE
Of course it's not my fault you got fired.

ADAM
Of . . . course. . . . And I'm not blaming you.

EVE
How gracious.

ADAM
What's done is done. It's no one's fault.

EVE
You're speaking in the passive voice. Like no one did anything; it just happened. But it didn't just happen. This action had agency. Someone made it happen.

ADAM
This action had agency? What are you, a grammar book?

EVE

Like you'd even know one if you saw one. And furthermore, it is someone's fault: Yours.

ADAM

You're treating me with contempt.

EVE

What?

ADAM

Contempt. Remember what Dr. Sydney said? Contempt is the one sure sign a marriage is over. Anger is fine, sadness is fine, whining is fine . . .

EVE

What do you mean—fine?

ADAM

Weren't you listening to Dr. Sydney? These are manageable emotions. But contempt is the point of no return.

EVE

How can you tell I'm feeling contempt and not anger?

ADAM

That twitch under your eye, in sector 9. It's a telltale sign.

EVE

You've divided my face into sectors?

ADAM

Weren't you listening to Dr. Sydney?

EVE

My face does not twitch.

ADAM

It's almost indistinguishable. Unless you know where to look. And

Eden ————————————— ✠ ————————————— 13

what to look for. And it seems to me that any wife who treats her husband with contempt on the morning after he gets fired—especially when she's the reason he gets fired—should not be twitching.

EVE

I thought you said it wasn't my fault.

ADAM

I was trying to be nice. I was afraid you'd feel guilty. I was being solicitous of your feelings.

EVE

More of Dr. Sydney's advice?

ADAM

What's wrong with that?

EVE

If you want to spend your time listening to a radio quack, fine with me.

ADAM

Twitch, twitch.

EVE

That's contempt for Dr. Sydney.

ADAM

And me.

EVE

Fine. And you.

ADAM

So you're saying this marriage is over?

EVE

I'm saying this conversation is over. One of us has to get to work.

ADAM

Ooh. Zinger. You don't even feel guilty.

EVE

"Guilt is a garbage emotion." Dr. Sydney.

ADAM

So you were listening.

Pause.

EVE

You never even said what you thought of the photo.

ADAM

Who took it?

EVE

What?

ADAM

Who took the photo? You see a nudie photo of your wife, that's the first thought that pops into your head. And it stays there a while. Until of course it's displaced by an e-mail from your boss saying you're fired.

EVE

I can't believe you opened it at work.

ADAM

I can't believe you sent it to me at work.

EVE

I didn't. I sent it to your personal account.

ADAM

But you sent it during business hours, so you knew I'd open it. Especially when you label it rated X. Triple X. Ex. Ex. Ex.

EVE

Which it wasn't.

ADAM

The perfect Eve. All those apples. Where'd you get the snake?

EVE

Photoshop.

ADAM

Who took the photo?

EVE

Simon.

ADAM

The scoundrel. You let him see you naked.

EVE

I was covered by apples. *Comme ça.*

> *SHE stands and poses flirtatiously as if for a photo shoot.*

As you said: the perfect Eve. Except for all these clothes. You did like it . . . didn't you?

ADAM

In the photo, the apples are strategically located. Now, not so much. Which means he must have helped you position the apples.

> *EVE breaks her flirtatious pose.*

Or he must have watched you do it yourself. Either way: the scoundrel.

EVE

I did it for you, you ingrate.

ADAM

You had another man position your apples—for me?

EVE

He's gay!

ADAM

So he says.

EVE

Please! If you're so concerned with other people seeing me nude, why would you open a triple-X photo of me at work where everyone can see your screen?

ADAM

Temptation, Eve.

EVE

And that's my fault?

ADAM

You've read the story. Eve's to blame.

EVE

Adam gets tossed out of the garden too! I can't believe you opened that picture in front of your whole office. I'd be embarrassed if I didn't look so damn good.

ADAM

Right.

EVE

You didn't think I looked good?

Silence.

You thought I looked fat? I didn't look fat. I pose naked in our garden for you, and all you can say is I look fat?

ADAM

I never said you look fat. You look skinny. Scrawny. Emaciated. You look like a concentration camp victim, a victim of ethnic cleansing. Even your apples are malnourished, dried up. You think that looks sensual? Guess again.

Eden ——————————————————— 17

EVE

Twitch, twitch. Twitch. I guess Dr. Sydney was right. This is it. The
end of Eden.

ADAM

Exactly. Just look at these weeds.

EVE

Apple trees are not weeds! They bear healthful, glorious fruits. And
ours are organic.

ADAM

What are we supposed to do with all these? They're going to fall
down and rot.

EVE

Make pie. That could be your next career. Pie man.

ADAM

I don't like pie.

EVE

Applesauce. Apple cider. Apple chutney. Apple brandy. I can already see
the jars lining the walls of the garage, the tourists stopping by to see
Adam and his apples in Eden. . . . Apples from the tree of truth . . .

ADAM

Knowledge. The tree of knowledge.

EVE

Well the truth is, you'd be good at it. And you need a job. You could
start tomorrow.

ADAM

You're not my boss.

EVE

Speaking of which. I'd like to see that e-mail. Would you forward it
to me?

ADAM

> Why?

EVE

> I want to see it. I've never heard of an esteemed employee getting fired by e-mail.

ADAM

> You don't believe me?

EVE

> Of course I believe you. Why wouldn't I believe you? Except supposedly you got fired for looking at a pornographic picture of me, and that photo was less revealing than the Altoids ads in *People* magazine.

ADAM

> It was suggestive.

EVE

> And furthermore, how would your boss even find out? He can't read the messages on your private account. And furthermore, you get spam all the time for erectile dysfunction drugs and escort services and God knows what else, so why suddenly is this one photo such a big deal?

ADAM

> You're accusing me of lying.

EVE

> You're not telling me the whole story. I could call Sam and see what really happened.

ADAM

> Sam! You must be kidding.

EVE

> Well his desk's next to yours. He must have seen the whole thing.

ADAM

   He saw the whole thing all right.

EVE

   What's that supposed to mean?

ADAM

   Call him. Go ahead. See what he says.

EVE

   What aren't you telling me?

ADAM

   Sam didn't like the picture.

EVE

   What does that mean?

ADAM

   Just what I said. Sam didn't like the picture. As soon as it popped
   up on the screen, he started mooing and railing about cows and
   chimeras and cardinal sin and other words that start with C, and . . .

EVE

   And what?

ADAM

   And I hit him.

EVE

   You what?

ADAM

   I punched him in the eye.

EVE

   That's why you got fired!

ADAM

    Violence in the workplace.

EVE

    Defending me?

ADAM

    Defending my wife.

EVE

    Really? That's so sexy. But Sam wouldn't say that about me. Sam
    loves me.

ADAM

    He didn't know it was you. He wasn't looking at your face, you
    know. I punched him in the eye, and he punched me in the rib. I've
    been trying to hide it, but it really hurts. I think it may be broken.

EVE

    You really did that for me? Then I apologize for getting you fired. I
    accept full responsibility.

ADAM

    Don't mention it.

EVE

    Maybe I should take the day off and . . .

ADAM

    One of us ought to earn some money. Gardens don't come cheap,
    you know.

EVE

    Simon can cover for me.

ADAM

    It was his idea, wasn't it.

EVE

    What? The picture? No. He just has the best camera. It was Dr. Sydney's idea.

ADAM

    Dr. Sydney!

EVE

    She did a show on "rekindling the flame" a few months ago when you were out of town. It took me a while because I wanted to lose weight for the photo.

ADAM

    What do you mean, rekindling? What do we need to rekindle? We have the perfect marriage.

EVE

    I've seen how you look at those gorgeous lady gardeners on HGTV. You don't look at me like that.

ADAM

    You don't want me to look at you like that; you want me to look at you with love, with respect, with adoration. Which I do, all the time, from the moment you awaken to the moment you fall asleep, and even in between. In fact my favorite time to watch you is when you're sleeping, when that secret smile on your face suggests you might be dreaming of me.

EVE

    God, Adam! You could have changed at least one word!

ADAM

    What?

EVE

    You got that off Dr. Sydney's website. Verbatim!

ADAM

    Sorry, but not everyone's a writer. And anyway, I mean it. I love looking at you.

EVE

I'm sorry you didn't like the picture.

ADAM

The picture's great. I love the picture.

EVE

I look like a saggy-boobed, middle-aged has-been. It's all right. You can say it. You might as well tell the truth. My apples *are* malnourished.

ADAM

They look great to me.

EVE

Well, it's nice of you to lie, but you're twitching in sector 12. You know what Dr. Sydney would say.

ADAM

That quack!

EVE

Simon and Sam and Dr. Sydney . . .

ADAM

They're jealous of our love.

EVE

They'll tear us apart.

ADAM

Let's never see them again—or listen to the radio.

EVE

I'll quit my job. We have each other and our garden. Let's never leave.

ADAM

We can live on love and apples.

EVE

> We can make applesauce together. We can write an apple cookbook.

ADAM

> We can write a diet book! That's where the real money is. *The Apple Diet: Advice from Eve.* Who better to sing the praises of the forbidden fruit?

EVE

> High in fiber, calcium, potassium. Tons of vitamin C. And they're delicious!

ADAM

> I'll eat to that.

> > *HE picks an apple, takes a bite, and offers it to Eve.*

> Have a bite?

> > *SHE bites the apple.*

END OF PLAY

SEX LESSONS

CHARACTERS

JACK   MID-30s. SILK BOXERS.
SALLY   MID-30s. LINGERIE.

Scene
A bedroom: a bed, a chair, a picture of Sally, an alarm clock.

AT RISE. SALLY holds a sheet around herself and sits at the edge of the bed. JACK reclines comfortably and holds a pack of cigarettes out to Sally.

JACK
Cigarette?

SALLY
No thanks. I don't smoke.

JACK
Let's try that again.
                    HE holds the pack of cigarettes out again.
Cigarette?

SALLY
Yeah. Okay.
                    SHE takes one.

JACK
Thank you.

SALLY
You're welcome.

JACK
No, you. Say "thank you." Take the cigarette, and say "thank you" with elegance and grace. Not "yeah."

SALLY

Thank you.

JACK

Now is not the time to be hunting down your panties. Relax. Stay a while. Say something nice. Something complimentary.

SALLY

That's a . . . nice photo on the wall. She's pretty.

JACK

Don't compliment the décor. Compliment me.

SALLY

You have very nice hair.

JACK

Tell me what a good time you've had.

SALLY

I've had a good time.

JACK

Sally. That is your name, right? Sally? You came to me for help. I'm trying to help you. But you don't seem to want to learn.

SALLY

I can do small talk. I didn't come to learn small talk.

JACK

There's nothing small about it. The post-coital conversation is essential. Or there'll be no second chance. Try again.

SALLY

Okay. That was great. Thanks.

JACK

Use my name. Jack . . .

SALLY

Thanks, Jack.

JACK

Tell me what you liked.

SALLY

Everything, Jack. You're incredible. Okay?

JACK

Tell me specifically.

SALLY

No. This is making me uncomfortable. I have to go.

JACK

We still have five minutes. Sally, you need to relax.

SALLY

How can I relax when all you do is criticize me?

JACK

I'm not criticizing. I'm teaching.

SALLY

I don't like your teaching style.

JACK

You seemed to like it twenty minutes ago.

SALLY

Now I see why you insist on getting paid in advance.

JACK

I have a 100-percent-satisfaction guarantee. If you don't feel you got your money's worth . . .

SALLY

No. No. I got my money's worth, okay? I just feel like . . . Why should I have to compliment you? It's ridiculous. You know you're amazing. I shouldn't have to say it. I want you to compliment me.

JACK

Then you'll have to earn it.

SALLY

You mean you didn't enjoy . . . ?

JACK

I mean I'm not going to be polite until you are. You'll have to take the first step here.

SALLY

Fine. Fine, Jack. I love what you did with your . . . and my . . . my . . . I never would have thought the ankle was an erogenous zone. You have the tongue of a snow leopard.

JACK

Much better.

SALLY

Thank you.

> *Pause.*

I'm waiting.

JACK

You have an ear fetish, don't you.

SALLY

That doesn't sound like a compliment. I'm going to leave. I have places to go.

> *SHE gets up, still wrapped in the sheet, and starts hunting for her clothing.*

JACK

Oh you do.

SALLY

Yes, I'm having dinner with my husband.

JACK

You're married?

SALLY

Of course. Why else would I be here?

JACK

Of course. Things getting stale. Husband's not an ear man?

SALLY

I didn't come here to be mocked. Where are my clothes?

JACK

We still have three and a half minutes.

SALLY

You've hidden my clothes.

JACK

Sally, please. Sit down.

SALLY

I need to take a shower.

JACK

I'll join you.

SALLY

No! . . . No thank you. Just . . .

JACK

Sit down and I'll give you a compliment.

SALLY

Please just give me my clothes.

JACK

Sit.

SALLY

Fine.

SHE sits on the chair.

JACK

On the bed. Sit by me.

SALLY

Fine!

SHE moves from the chair to the bed.

JACK

You're really very beautiful . . .

SALLY

But?

JACK

Don't interrupt. Your legs are long and muscular, and what you do with your toes is outrageous.

SALLY

You're mocking me.

JACK

I'm perfectly sincere.

SALLY

Is "outrageous" a good thing?

JACK

Absolutely. You're supple, limber, and lithe. These are very good things. You bend easily.

SALLY

Sometimes it hurts.

JACK

And then you scream, which is a nice touch, too.

> *A buzzer buzzes, or a bell rings, loudly. JACK stands, turns off the alarm, puts on a robe, and plops himself into the chair. SALLY relaxes.*

Whoa! That was fun. Did you have fun? That was amazing. I feel liberated. Invigorated. Don't you feel invigorated?

SALLY

I feel like I've been dipped in mud.

JACK

That's sexy.

SALLY

Like I need to be sanded down and bleached.

JACK

You're saying you didn't have a good time? You seemed to have a good time. Until the talking. Then you got crabby.

SALLY

Jack's great in bed, but what a creep.

JACK

He's just doing his job.

SALLY

What kind of person gives sex lessons for a living?

JACK

It's not "a living." It's just part-time. Consider it his contribution to society. He's helping make the world a better place, one pathetically needy female at a time.

SALLY

You don't need to insult Sally.

JACK

Don't take it personally.

SALLY

Of course not.

JACK

You haven't even seen her in years. It's not like you're still friends.

SALLY

We were never really friends.

JACK

You're nothing like her.

SALLY

Nothing? What about my legs and toes? And what you said about my being limber? Supple? And lithe?

JACK

That was Jack.

SALLY

So it wasn't true?

JACK

Of course it was true. But it wasn't me saying it, and it wasn't about you. It was Jack and Sally.

SALLY

But you've never met either of them! Why would you want to be such a creep?

JACK

It's my birthday.

SALLY

That's supposed to explain it?

JACK

    When it's your birthday, you choose. Today's my turn. Anyway, you told me about the sex lessons.

SALLY

    I know. Isn't it funny. It was 15 years ago, and I can't get it out of my head. But I'd never want to be Sally.

JACK

    What kind of person takes sex lessons?

SALLY

    She was always competitive, got A's in every class. I guess everything was school to her, even sex.

JACK

    Do you think she got an A?

SALLY

    I don't know. You're the one doing the grading.

JACK

    Not me. Jack. And I meant the real Sally. Your friend.

SALLY

    I don't want to think about it.

JACK

    Neither do I.

SALLY

    It's too pathetic.

JACK

    I know.

SALLY

    I'm glad we're not like that.

JACK

I know.

SALLY

Not that I would mind a little praise every now and then. But I do have self-confidence. I know I'm good. I know I don't need lessons to keep my husband interested.

Pause.

JACK

Of course not.

SALLY

And that you really are an ear man.

JACK

Of . . . course.

SALLY

You're not?

JACK

No, no . . . I mean yes. I am. If you like it, I like it.

SALLY

You mean you're really into toes?

JACK

It may be just a phase.

SALLY

You could have told me. You could be more assertive.

JACK

You don't think I'm assertive?

SALLY

You need to say what you like.

JACK

Like Jack?

SALLY

Oh, God. I didn't mean that.

JACK

I think maybe you did. See you learned something about yourself today. Didn't you. It makes you more objective.

SALLY

Just thinking I may have thought that makes me feel like I have fungal spores in my brain.

JACK

Sexy.

SALLY

Not to mention my more vital organs.

JACK

Sounds like it's about time for that shower.

HE picks up the alarm clock.

Ten more minutes? It is my birthday.

SALLY

Your present was one hour. Can't we just be ourselves? Don't you want to be with me?

JACK

Of course. I want to be with. You. You're supple, limber, and lithe. . . . Your legs are long and muscular . . .

SALLY

That's not me. That's Sally.

JACK

And you think snow leopard tongues are sexy. Mee-ow.

SALLY

Not me. Sally.

JACK

She's hot, isn't she? She must be hot. . . . I think I may be falling for Sally. She's petulant and humble.

SALLY

You've never met Sally. You wouldn't like Sally.

JACK

She's everything I've ever wanted in a woman.

SALLY

I'm everything you've ever wanted in a woman. You called Sally "pathetically needy."

JACK

Maybe I'm what she needs.

SALLY

Jack didn't like Sally. Jack would prefer me.

JACK

You know, you're right. Jack would.

SALLY

Jack's better in bed than you.

JACK

Mee-ow.

SALLY

It's almost time for your birthday dinner.

JACK

Maybe it's time to swap, to switch. To trade. You take Jack, I keep Sally.

SALLY
    You can't keep Sally. Sally's gone.

JACK
    But I'm not ready to say goodbye.

End of Play

HENRY

CHARACTERS

> HIM
> HER

> *Scene*
> *A room. A bed with two blankets, one spread over*
> *the bed and the other folded into a square. There is*
> *nothing else in the room. The light may have an eerie*
> *quality. Props should appear magically, maybe lowered*
> *by pulleys from above.*
>
> *AT RISE. HE discovers her standing in the doorway.*
> *THEY embrace and kiss passionately. HE closes the*
> *door, steps back and admires her.*

HIM
> You look fantastic.

HER
> So do you.

HIM
> You haven't changed a bit.

HER
> Since yesterday?

HIM
> Since last year.

HER
> Last year?

HIM
> We haven't seen each other in a year.

HER
> We haven't?

HIM

No.

HER

How can that be? We're engaged. We just picked out our china pattern. It seems like yesterday.

HIM

No, I ran off.

HER

Didn't like the Wedgewood?

HIM

With another woman.

HER

That's right. You did.

HIM

And you burned all my stuff.

HER

That's right. I did. I burned it all. And now you live here? You left me for this? It's not very nice.

HIM

I've come back. This is my new place. These are my new digs.

HER

It's just a bed.

HIM

I rented it. I don't have anything else.

HER

Why not?

HIM

You burned it.

HER

That's right. I did. And you deserved it.

HIM

That's right. I did. I'm sorry.

HER

You're sorry?

HIM

Yes, and I've come back.

HER

I always knew that you'd come crawling back. But I can't take you back. Not after the way you've hurt me. I feel the pain in my heart. And my stomach. My lungs. My legs. How could you?

HIM

I didn't mean to.

HER

You didn't even leave a note.

HIM

I didn't want to hurt you.

HER

But now?

HIM

Now we are going on a picnic.

HER

A picnic? I've always wanted to go on a picnic! You've been promising a picnic for a long time. Where are we going? To the mountains? To the park? To the lake?

HIM

Right here.

> *HE takes the folded blanket and spreads it on the bed. SHE helps straighten it out.*

HER

Right here? We can't have a picnic right here.

HIM

Why not?

> *A picnic basket appears. HE puts it on the blanket.*

Here it is.

HER

Oh good, a picnic. We're going on a picnic!

HIM

Isn't this romantic?

> *A small vase of flowers appears. HE puts it in the center of the blanket.*

Isn't this romantic.

HER

This is so romantic.

> *HE removes sandwiches, napkins, and bottled water from the picnic basket and lays them on the blanket. HE unwraps the sandwiches and hands one to her.*

HIM

Your favorite. Smoked turkey with Brie. On Tuscan bread. With sprouts and sunflower seeds and sun-dried tomatoes.

HER

My favorite. This is beautiful. I've always wanted a picnic.

> *THEY each take a bite of sandwich.*

HIM

We also have bottled water. With bubbles.

HER

My favorite.

HIM

So you're not mad?

HER

Mad? Why would I be mad? This is the best picnic ever.

The sound of a baby crying, but just for a brief second.

What was that?

HIM

What was what?

HER

I thought I heard a baby.

HIM

Oh?

HER

I'm always hearing babies lately.

HIM

Oh.

HER

It must be hormonal.

HIM

I owe you an apology.

HER

For what?

HIM

For leaving you.

HER

For leaving me? When?

HIM

I've been gone six months.

HER

Six months? But we just put a deposit on the banquet hall. It seems like yesterday.

HIM

I left you.

SHE walks away from the picnic.

HER

That's right. You did. Ran off with another woman. How could you do that? You've caused me so much pain. My heart. My lungs. My toes.

HIM

You burned my stuff.

HER

All of it. Huge bonfire. Roasted marshmallows. But I couldn't eat them. I felt ill.

HIM

We were going to get married. I gave you a ring.

HER

Do you want your ring back? Is that why you invited me here?

HIM

Didn't you burn it? I just assumed.

HER

Diamonds don't burn. I tried. I guess you want it back. Well, you can't have it.

HIM

No, you keep it.

HER

If you don't want it, neither do I. Here. It's yours.

> *SHE removes the ring from her finger and hands it to him. HE takes it and inspects it.*

HIM

It's smaller than I remembered.

HER

It is small.

HIM

But it's pretty.

HER

It's okay.

HIM

Now you're hurt?

HER

Now? It's been two years. Two years of hurt. You ran away. Didn't even leave a note. And suddenly here you are with smoked turkey and Brie. I don't eat that anymore, you know. I'm a vegetarian. And lactose intolerant. You don't know a thing.

> *HE wraps the blanket around the picnic and ties it up. The picnic somehow disappears.*

HIM

I think you should keep the ring.

HER

No thanks. We broke up. Dear Abby says to give the ring back. So does my mother. And besides, it reminds me of you.

HIM

Is that so bad?

HER

The pain is in my heart. My lungs. My hands. How could you leave me?

HIM

For another woman.

HER

For another woman. And you didn't even leave a note.

HIM

I didn't want to hurt you.

HER

And so you didn't leave a note?

HIM

I left you because she was pregnant. And I wanted to do the right thing.

HER

The right thing.

HIM

You always talked about children, and I always said no. But here I was having one. So I thought it best not to tell you.

HER

You didn't want me to be jealous.

HIM

So I went to Minneapolis.

HER

I've never been to Minneapolis.

HIM

I couldn't help myself.

HER

You couldn't.

HIM

She was like a siren singing for a sailor, but I wasn't smart enough
to plug my ears. So I followed her. Fell for her. Impregnated her.

HER

Against your will.

HIM

I had no will. She raped me, shackled me, kept me prisoner. Forced
me to have her baby.

HER

But you're a man.

HIM

Such things can happen.

HER

So I've heard, but I can't imagine.

HIM

She has magical powers. And the tongue of a cat.

HER

I don't want to hear about her tongue.

HIM

Then I left her.

HER

What about the baby?

HIM

She didn't want it. She laid it out with the trash one morning at daybreak. That broke the spell, and together we escaped.

HER

We?

HIM

Me and Henry.

HER

Henry?

HIM

My son.

> *A doll appears. HE takes it and holds it like a baby. A brief baby's cry, as before.*

HER

I knew I heard a baby. He's beautiful.

HIM

He has six toes.

HER

On each foot?

HIM

Yes.

HER

How romantic.

HIM

But only one nose.

HER

That's for the best.

HIM

So will you marry me and be his mother?

HER

Of course not. I'm already someone's mother. I have a baby of my own.

HIM

You do?

> *A second doll appears, accompanied by the sound of a brief baby's cry. SHE takes it and holds it like a baby.*

HER

Oh, yes. She's lovely too. And she also has six toes.

HIM

On each foot.

HER

And one nose.

HIM

How old is she?

HER

She's the same age as Henry.

HIM

Well then she must be mine.

HER

She might not.

HIM

But we were together . . .

HER

But Henry's not mine. So there your logic falls apart.

HIM

 I think they like each other.

HER

 I think they have gas.

HIM

 I love you, you know.

HER

 Yes, I know. But I'm not magical, so I can't keep you.

HIM

 But I love you.

HER

 You're not very strong.

HIM

 I can lift the bed.

HER

 Please don't. That's not what I meant.

HIM

 We could live happily ever after: you, me, Henry, and . . .

HER

 Henrietta.

HIM

 Henrietta?

HER

 Yes.

HIM

 Yes, you'll marry me?

HER

    Yes, her name is Henrietta.

        The dolls disappear. HE kneels and offers her the ring.

HIM

    Please will you marry me?

HER

    I always knew you'd come crawling back. But I can't take you back. Not after the way you've hurt me. I feel the pain in my heart. My lungs. My toes. All six of them.

HIM

    But we have the ring, the china pattern, the banquet hall.

HER

    We had those things, but now they're gone.

HIM

    We still have the ring.

HER

    That's not the same ring. I got it in a gumball machine. It's made of peppermint candy.

        HE puts the ring in his mouth and swallows.

HIM

    Delicious.

        The sound of a baby crying, once, briefly.

HER

    Now everything is gone.

        The sound of the baby crying begins again and rapidly intensifies. His doll reappears. The noise seems to be coming from the doll. HE does not know what to do. HE holds the doll up high, gently shakes it, and tries to hand it to her. SHE watches him calmly but does not move.

END OF PLAY

I LOVE YOU TERRIBLY

CHARACTERS

> HIM
> HER

Setting
An empty space.

Playwright's Note
I picture this play performed as a stylized dance like a
tango, with shifts in attitude and direction coinciding
with shifts between beats, though I leave such choices
entirely to the discretion of the director—so there are
no stage directions. Or it could be a radio play.

HIM

> I won't say "Mama" when I die. I'll be asking for my dog.

HER

> You'll be asking for me. Begging for me.

HIM

> Begging you to stop killing me. To take your claws off my throat.

HER

> And your dog's claws?

HIM

> They'd be scratching your heart, if you had one.

HER

> I lost my heart when I met you.

HIM

> You lost your heart to me.

HER

> Ace of hearts.

HIM
Queen of hearts.

HER
Go fish.

HIM
I love you terribly.

HER
Every time you say that, I love you less.

HIM
I love you terribly.

HER
I wish you'd love me well instead.

HIM
I love you like hell. And you love me—

HER
Like hell.

HIM
The perfect couple: you and me.

HER
And your dog.

HIM
I don't have a dog.

HER
And your mama?

HIM
I don't have a mama.

HER

Everybody has a mama.

HIM

Not me. I'm sprung from the loins of a live oak tree.

HER

Then the live oak's your mama. Except trees don't have loins.

HIM

Live oaks are exceptional.

HER

Live oaks are from Louisiana; you're from Long Island.

HIM

Rhode Island.

HER

Last week you said Long Island.

HIM

That's what you love about me, that I'm ever-changing.

HER

That is not what I love about you.

HIM

That I'm unpredictable.

HER

You mean unreliable?

HIM

You love that you can never really know me, that you cannot pin me down.

HER

I find that annoying.

HIM

And you love our spiky banter.

HER

I find that exhausting.

HIM

Then what do you love about me?

HER

Your hair. I love your wavy dark hair. The way it shines, the way it smells, the way it feels when I run my fingers through your tresses—your hot, musky, feral fur.

HIM

My hair?

HER

And your eyes. Such a unique hue of blue.

HIM

"Caspian See."

HER

Caspian Sea?

HIM

See. S.E.E. It's a pun. That's what it says on the box. Tinted lenses.

HER

That's not the color of your eyes?

HIM

Not exactly.

HER

Then you're not exactly the man I love.

HIM

I am when I'm wearing them.

HER

That's true. Now say what you love about me.

HIM

I don't know. I never really thought about it.

HER

Then think about it.

HIM

But love's intuitive. And emotional. It's not prone to rationalization. It just is.

HER

Maybe it's my dancer's legs?

HIM

No.

HER

My champagne-coupe breasts?

HIM

No.

HER

No!

HIM

Of course I love them, but I don't love you for them.

HER

Give me one reason you love me. Right now.

HIM

I love that you don't cry, no matter what I say.

HER

Crying makes me thirsty.

HIM

Really?

HER

I hate to dehydrate. And crying takes me past the water stage.

HIM

The water stage?

HER

When water helps. You get to that point when you really just need an icy cold Coke, and I don't want to do that to my body.

HIM

What if you're sad?

HER

Why would I be sad?

HIM

You might be sad if you watched a sappy movie with a poignant soundtrack and a gloomy ending. You might be sad if you forgot your favorite ski hat on an uptown bus. You might be sad if you were bitten by a rabid squirrel.

HER

I might.

HIM

And then would you cry?

HER

I might not.

HIM

Won't you cry at our wedding?

HER

Our wedding? You want to marry me?

HIM

I thought you'd never ask.

HER

I never will.

HIM

What if I asked? Would you marry me?

HER

Are you asking me to marry you, or are you asking what if?

HIM

What's the difference?

HER

Who's the alpha.

HIM

What do you mean?

HER

If you ask me to marry you, the choice is mine. If you ask me what if, the choice is yours.

HIM

So that's why women don't ask.

HER

Don't ask who? You?

HIM

Men always ask. Still. Even with a woman running for president.

HER

She didn't win.

HIM

Do you think she asked him?

HER

Of course not. She's no fool.

HIM

I'm glad you don't wear pant-suits.

HER

I might.

HIM

When?

HER

At our wedding.

HIM

Our wedding? You want to marry me?

HER

I'll have to think about it.

HIM

But I wasn't—

HER

I'll have to sleep on it. It's a major decision.

HIM

And you hardly know me.

HER

What would our life be like if I married you?

HIM

A passionate ballet with dips and turns, slow rhythms and fox trots,
pirouettes and cha-cha-chas. We'd always hear background music in

our heads.

HER
Happy music?

HIM
Sometimes.

HER
And other times?

HIM
Sad little ditties, melancholy melodies, tragic operettas. That's life.

HER
What would my name be if I married you?

HIM
Daisy.

HER
My last name?

HIM
Daisy.

HER
Daisy Daisy?

HIM
If you marry me, you can be anyone you want to be.

HER
Just like you are?

HIM
Unpredictable.

HER

Unreliable.

HIM

We'll have the ceremony in the shade of the live oak tree.

HER

In Rhode Island?

HIM

In Rhodesia.

HER

Rhodesia no longer exists.

HIM

Then it's the perfect spot for a fairy-tale wedding.

HER

And we'll live happily ever after.

HIM

Except for the dog.

HER

You don't have a dog.

HIM

I don't but I will, and I'll love her with all my heart.

HER

Why?

HIM

Because she'll eat sliced mangoes and bark at hummingbirds in late summer.

HER

And I'll be jealous and scratch your heart out?

HIM

I won't say "Daisy" when I die. I'll be asking for my dog instead.

HER

You want to make me cry?

HIM

Will you?

HER

Not today.

HIM

Then let's tie the knot today.

HER

You love me terribly.

HIM

I do.

HER

Every time you say that, I love you less.

HIM

I do.

END OF PLAY

TILL DEATH

CHARACTERS

JULIAN   MALE, 40s–50s.
FELICITY   FEMALE, 40s.

Scene
Julian's study: a desk with chair, armchair, and reading lamp. Neat.

AT RISE. JULIAN sits in the armchair reading a book. FELICITY enters.

FELICITY
>What if I were dead?

JULIAN
>I'm reading.

FELICITY
>I mean it. I might die.

JULIAN
>You will definitely die.

FELICITY
>I might die before you. You think you'll die first, but I could die any day. It would be tragic: I'm healthy and young. But anything could happen: a random bullet from a drive-by shooting, a funnel cloud swirling with sharp debris, a fall from a slippery cliff when we're hiking in the rain.

JULIAN
>Especially if I push you.

FELICITY
>I'm serious.

JULIAN
>You bought those new boots for the traction.

FELICITY

Still sometimes I slide a little. Wet leaves are slick. I could fall, break my neck, crush my skull. Even though I exercise three times a week, eat a high-fiber diet, and take multi-vitamins every day, I could die. My luck could run out. And then: What would you do?

JULIAN

I'd read.

FELICITY

Seriously.

JULIAN

I'm almost finished with this poem.

FELICITY

That poem will be around forever. I might not.

JULIAN

Okay. Fine. My wife is dying, so to hell with my book.

HE inserts a bookmark and closes the book. SHE takes it from him and clutches it to her chest.

FELICITY

I'm not dying. I just asked: What if I did? What would you do? Haven't you considered the possibility?

JULIAN

Would you mind putting my book on the desk? I don't want the cover to get ruined.

FELICITY

My hands are not sweaty.

SHE puts the book on the desk, inspects her hands briefly, and wipes them on her pants.

Plus I'd think you'd be grateful for any memento of me once I'm dead.

SHE looks at the book on the desk.

Robert Browning? That's a little macabre.

JULIAN

Are you on some sort of new diet pill again?

FELICITY

Meaning what? You think I'm fat?

JULIAN

I think you're high. If you're going to stay, at least sit down.

> SHE sits in the chair at his desk, at first tentatively but then as if it's hers.

FELICITY

Here? I'm allowed to sit at your desk? It's so grand and important. But there's nothing on it to play with—no pen caps or paper clips . . .

JULIAN

Your energy is distracting.

FELICITY

I haven't slept. I'm obsessed with my death. I asked you a question: What would you do?

JULIAN

I'd grieve.

FELICITY

And after that?

JULIAN

I'd grieve some more.

FELICITY

And then?

JULIAN

Then? Then I'd sell your car. And my car. And buy a Porsche Boxster S, two hundred and ninety horsepower, metallic malachite green. And I'd drive it up and down the shore-line roads, looking for an unimpeded view of the summer sun setting on the sea, and

when I found it, assuming you'd designated me as the beneficiary
of your retirement account and life insurance, not to mention
all those sick days you never use, I'd build my new domicile
on titanium stilts, with glass walls, umbrellaed balconies, and
pearly white floors. Then I'd retire from my job, take up orchid
gardening, and marry someone sweet and young who'd let me read
in peace.

FELICITY
You'd remarry?

JULIAN
I thought you'd want me to be happy.

FELICITY
Marrying some stranger would make you happy?

JULIAN
Would it have to be a stranger? I was envisioning Lanie Rieves.

FELICITY
She's already married.

JULIAN
So am I.

FELICITY
How are you planning to get rid of Tom?

JULIAN
I haven't even figured out how to get rid of you.

FELICITY
I can't believe you think she's pretty.

JULIAN
I don't. I just assume she's good in bed.

FELICITY

It's hard to believe I once fell in love with your sense of humor, Julian.

JULIAN

That was a long time ago. Maybe you've changed, Felicity.

FELICITY

Maybe I've changed! Just look at yourself.

JULIAN

I still look the same as I did in college. I wear the same size pants.

FELICITY

Sure you do. Since the chemo.

JULIAN

Same size pants, same size shirt, same size hat.

FELICITY

You never wore a hat before the chemo.

Pause.

Julian, what are you going to do if the cancer comes back?

JULIAN

I don't know.

FELICITY

What do you mean you don't know?

JULIAN

I. Don't. Know.

FELICITY

You've already picked out your dream car and dream house and dream wife for when I die, but if your cancer comes back, you have no contingency plan?

JULIAN

Because you're not going to die. You'll live to be a hundred and four.

FELICITY

That's too old. I don't want to be a feeble, lonely woman surrounded by cats. I'm allergic to cats.

JULIAN

You're likely to outgrow that allergy as your immunity changes. You can have as many cats as you like.

FELICITY

I don't like cats.

JULIAN

I know. Neither do I. Didn't the doctor make you promise to believe I'd live forever? That's what supportive spouses are supposed to do.

FELICITY

Promise not to leave me.

JULIAN

I promise.

FELICITY

I mean it. I need you.

JULIAN

Aha! She admits it. Porphyria worships me.

FELICITY

You're so romantic. Now what? You strangle me, like in the poem?

JULIAN

No, I trust you.

Pause.

I plan to spend eternity with you.

FELICITY

You mean we'll be buried together. What if one of us remarries? Then what happens to those burial plots we bought in Sedona? Do we make room for number three? I refuse to be buried with Lanie Rieves.

JULIAN

My nightmare's you selling your half on eBay to a retired sumo wrestler. I'd have to spend eternity with him.

FELICITY

My mother ordered my father to remarry. On her deathbed. She made him promise not to grieve too long, to go out and find a wife.

JULIAN

She loved him.

FELICITY

I can't relate to that. I can't imagine you with anyone else. It would drive me insane.

JULIAN

That's because you're not dying. You're beautiful, vibrant, healthy, and young. Your mother disintegrated slowly over time. She had time to think about death seriously. With gravitas.

FELICITY

If you married Lanie Rieves, I'd haunt you like Heathcliff.

JULIAN

That's my girl.

FELICITY

I'd come back as a crow, sharpen my beak, and peck out her eyes.

> Pause.

Would you haunt me?

JULIAN

You mean if you remarried?

FELICITY
Yes.

JULIAN
I don't know.

FELICITY
You don't know anything.

JULIAN
No. I wouldn't. I would not haunt you.

FELICITY
You'd want me to be happy?

JULIAN
Yes.

FELICITY
Well I wouldn't be. I couldn't be.

JULIAN
Good.

FELICITY
Good?

JULIAN
I'm not really that noble.

FELICITY
Or you don't love me that much.

JULIAN
Exactly.

FELICITY
Which is it?

Pause.

You don't know.

JULIAN

    I don't love you that much.

FELICITY

    I knew it.

    Pause.

    I'd have pegged you for cherry red.

    Pause.

    The Porsche. Malachite green?

JULIAN

    Metallic malachite green. Red's too obvious.

FELICITY

    I don't guess we can afford one?

JULIAN

    Not the S series. Besides, they're gas guzzlers.

FELICITY

    And the house on the beach? I thought you hate sand.

JULIAN

    In my fantasy, it's sand-free.

FELICITY

    And Lanie Rieves? You used to have better taste.

JULIAN

    That was a long time ago. Maybe I have changed.

FELICITY

    And maybe you haven't. You're still reading the same old poem.

    SHE picks up the book, opens it.

JULIAN
Don't.

FELICITY
You used to love when I'd read poetry aloud.

JULIAN
Please. Don't.

SHE skims the poem, closes the book.

FELICITY
It's grisly and sweet. Does it make you think of me?

JULIAN
Your hair's too short. Your eyes aren't blue. And you fidget too much.

FELICITY
So did she.

JULIAN
Not anymore.

FELICITY
Now she sits still. The ideal woman. She'd let you read.

JULIAN
I wouldn't be able to concentrate with her head drooped on my shoulder.

FELICITY
And she wouldn't be good in bed.

JULIAN
You never know. Some people are into that.

FELICITY
Not much of a fantasy. Death.

Pause.

The doctor said your remission could last forever.

JULIAN

Honesty's more interesting. More refreshing.

FELICITY

Her eyes are laughing even after she's dead. She's fixed in her
moment of bliss. What happens next?

Pause.

Do you think they're still sitting there, her cheek burning bright
in the afterglow of strangulation? You could write "Porphyria: The
Sequel." A narrative poem about a man and his fetish, part 2. What
happens if and when said man comes to his senses? Or, better yet,
what happens when the police come looking for the asphyxiated
blonde?

Pause.

Or, better yet: I could write it. I'll sit here at your desk and pretend
to be the poet. What if he's gone completely mad? What if he has
no memory of what he's done? What if he can't live without her?
. . . What if she's not really dead?

JULIAN

Or what if he's about to die himself? His internal organs rotting
with disease . . .

FELICITY

And he can't bear to think of her in the arms of another man. . . .

JULIAN

Even though if he really loved her, he'd want her to be happy.

FELICITY

He's just too tidy to leave any loose ends.

JULIAN

So he ends her life just as he expects his own to end . . .

FELICITY

Only then the old doctor arrives in the middle of the night, having braved the storm to deliver the happy news: The diagnosis was wrong! Our man will live! But then he looks at his love and asks himself: What have I done?

JULIAN

And realizes he's now free to marry Lanie Rieves.

FELICITY

Except that she's still married to Tom . . .

JULIAN

And he'll be spending the next forty years in jail.

FELICITY

Unless of course capital punishment is still legal.

                    Pause.

JULIAN

Not much of a fantasy. Death.

FELICITY

It's forever that's the fantasy.

END OF PLAY

PRECIPICE

CHARACTERS

ELANNA   FEMALE. 40S. LOVELY. WEARS A NIGHTGOWN.
DUSHA   MALE. SAME AGE. FULLY DRESSED, WITH AN
OVERCOAT.

Scene
A room with a bed and a nightstand. A door leads
outside. An empty wine bottle sits on the nightstand.

AT RISE. ELANNA sits on the bed. DUSHA
stands; sometimes HE paces. EACH holds a glass of
red wine. ELANNA sips now and then. DUSHA
never drinks; HE may at times place his glass on the
nightstand. THEY never touch.

ELANNA
> The woman spoke with a heavy accent and said her name was
> Lucrezia. She said she was calling to ask my "scent." She would be
> meeting me at the airport and would need some way to recognize me.

DUSHA
> "My scent?" you asked.

ELANNA
> "Perfume," she explained.

DUSHA
> "I just use soap," you replied.

ELANNA
> She sighed audibly.

DUSHA
> You don't know anyone named Lucrezia.

ELANNA
> You don't like the name? I can change it.

DUSHA
No, it's perfect. It's Italian. You were flying to Italy.

ELANNA
Was I?

Pause.

Remember that hike in Umbria when I stood at the edge of the precipice?

DUSHA
Despite your fear of heights.

ELANNA
I looked down at the treetops below and thought:

DUSHA
"Imagine all the skeletons down there. People fall, people jump. Animals fall, animals jump . . . and who would find them?"

ELANNA
And then you said:

DUSHA
"Animals don't jump. Not on purpose. Animals want to live."

ELANNA
Humans are animals.

DUSHA
Not anymore. They've devolved.

ELANNA
They?

Pause.

I don't want to die.

DUSHA

You don't.

ELANNA

I would if it meant we could spend eternity together—in more than a literal, mud-infested way.

DUSHA

But you don't believe in that.

ELANNA

I took a drive in the country today: narrow roads snaking 'round creeks, cutting through valleys, climbing mountains toward the sky.

DUSHA

You sat elegantly straight and hummed along to the soundtrack from *Tosca*, wishing you knew the words.

ELANNA

After a while, I spotted a white cross planted in the ground like a marker at a military cemetery, surrounded by snapdragons and speedwell and sweet peas. A combat grave in this time of peace. I stopped and read the inscription. The name was yours: Dusha.

DUSHA

It's a common name.

ELANNA

I know.

DUSHA

You're exhausted.

ELANNA

The good news is that it's time for bed. The bad news is that I'll dream I've lost you, and I'll miss you. I wish I could somehow convince my sleeping self that you'll be in bed beside me when I awaken—but my sleeping self's no fool.

DUSHA

   Lie back and rest.

ELANNA

   Let's talk more about Umbria. That was the day you saw the wild
   boar.

DUSHA

   You'd stopped to examine a porcupine quill.

ELANNA

   She bared her teeth when she saw you.

DUSHA

   Defending her young.

ELANNA

   So you retreated. Or she'd have mauled you.

DUSHA

   I saw it in her eyes.

ELANNA

   What do you see in my eyes?

DUSHA

   That porcupine quill.

ELANNA

   I used it to tie back my hair.

DUSHA

   And then you lost it, like so many things.

ELANNA

   When I landed at Fiumicino, a woman approached me, sniffing. She
   had a surprisingly small nose.

DUSHA

"Soap," she said. And then she said your name, "Elanna."

ELANNA

And she drove me to you. In her little Italian car. A . . . Lamborghini
. . . or a Maserati . . .

DUSHA

More likely a Fiat.

ELANNA

An Alfa Romeo. To take me to Romeo.

DUSHA

Don't idealize me.

ELANNA

You never meant to hurt me.

DUSHA

I almost never meant to hurt you.

ELANNA

She sped along the *autostrada*, beak-first.

DUSHA

You said her nose was small.

ELANNA

She sped along the *autostrada*. I sat in the back seat.

DUSHA

The Fiat had only two seats.

ELANNA

I sat beside her and watched the speedometer, wondering how one
hundred forty kilometers translated to miles.

DUSHA
You felt intimidated.

ELANNA
I felt invigorated. I love to drive.

DUSHA
You weren't driving.

ELANNA
You're contradicting me.

DUSHA
You hate to drive.

ELANNA
I never said it was fact.

DUSHA
It's time for me to leave.

ELANNA
Please stay. I'll tell it true.

DUSHA
She delivered you to me.

ELANNA
Lucrezia dropped me at the *duomo* where you waited on the steps.

DUSHA
That's how we first met.

ELANNA
It was love at first sight.

DUSHA
Then I took you for a picnic. I spread a blanket on a precipice. We ate Gorgonzola and *sopressata*, and drank a dark red wine.

ELANNA

A Chianti.

DUSHA

A Corvina.

ELANNA

And we lived happily ever after.

DUSHA

The end.

ELANNA

What happened to Lucrezia?

DUSHA

She drove off into the sunset.

ELANNA

Is that where you'll go?

DUSHA

The sun set long ago.

ELANNA

I've never been to Italy.

DUSHA

Lay your head on the pillow.

ELANNA

I took a drive in the country last month: narrow roads snaking
'round creeks, cutting through valleys, climbing mountains toward
the sky. I sat elegantly straight and hummed along to the soundtrack
from *Tosca*, wishing I knew the words.

DUSHA

I know. I was there.

ELANNA

After a while, we spotted a precipice surrounded by snapdragons and speedwell and sweet peas. We stopped and spread a picnic blanket.

DUSHA

We ate Gorgonzola and *sopressata*, and drank a dark red wine. It stained your lips.

ELANNA

That was the day you saw the dog.

DUSHA

We wandered down a trail to look at wildflowers. You fell behind, distracted by sweet William.

ELANNA

I heard the mongrel growl.

DUSHA

Like a mother boar who sees her piglets in peril, she ran towards the transgressor.

ELANNA

She bared her fangs when she saw you. So you retreated. Or she'd have mauled you. You saw it in her eyes.

DUSHA

What do you see in my eyes?

ELANNA

Tar. Quicksand. Blackberry syrup.

DUSHA

You're mired in memory.

ELANNA

I took some pills.

DUSHA

I know. Tell me about tomorrow.

ELANNA

I start to stir with the first light and reflect upon my dreams. I remember you were here, I regret some things I said, I wonder who drank the wine.

DUSHA

Still mired.

ELANNA

I take a drive in the country: narrow roads snaking 'round creeks—

DUSHA

Drive elsewhere.

ELANNA

I drive to Italy.

DUSHA

You'd need to fly.

ELANNA

I flap my wings.

DUSHA

You'd soar.

ELANNA

I ride the wind through wispy clouds and silver raindrops, sailing above hilltops and steeples, promontories and cliffs . . .

DUSHA

That's lovely.

ELANNA

Then I gaze at the world below and imagine all the skeletons. All the humans and animals who jumped or fell or were mauled by dogs. I used to like dogs.

DUSHA

There wasn't any dog.

ELANNA

And there wasn't any picnic.

DUSHA

There was only the precipice.

ELANNA

On a crisp autumn day. Where did I lose the porcupine needle?

DUSHA

It fell from your hair as you flew over a forest.

ELANNA

You didn't love me enough.

DUSHA

You're speaking in the past.

ELANNA

Are you with her when you're not with me?

DUSHA

Whatever helps you sleep.

ELANNA

In more than a mud-infested way?

DUSHA

You don't believe in that.

ELANNA

I hid in the leaves of a sycamore.

DUSHA

By a rippling creek, on a warm spring day.

ELANNA

I smelled of soap.

DUSHA

And speedwell.

ELANNA

And *sopressata*.

DUSHA

There wasn't any her.

ELANNA

There isn't any you.

DUSHA

I know.

ELANNA

I took some pills.

DUSHA

You don't believe in that.

ELANNA

Not many.

DUSHA

You'll flush the rest tomorrow.

ELANNA

Before my flight.

DUSHA

You promise.

ELANNA

The good news is that it's time for bed.

DUSHA

Don't forget to lock the door behind me.

ELANNA

The door locks automatically.

DUSHA

Lock the deadbolt. Please. I want you to be safe.

ELANNA

Then how will you get back in?

> *Pause. DUSHA exits through the door and closes it behind him. HE takes his wine glass with him. ELANNA lays her head on the pillow as if to sleep. Her glass is empty.*

END OF PLAY